THE BLACK HAWK SONGS

For Marilyn,
Best wishes
and good luck on
all your songs.
—Michael
Oct 9, 1985

The Black Hawk Songs

MICHAEL BORICH

University of Illinois Press

Urbana Chicago London

Library of Congress Cataloging in Publication Data

Borich, Michael, 1949–
  The Black Hawk songs.

  1. Black Hawk, Sauk chief, 1767–1838 — Poetry.
I. Title.
PS3552.0753B5   811'.5'4   74-23379
ISBN 0-252-00471-X
ISBN 0-252-00528-7 pbk.

For my parents,
and for Lynn

Contents

Last Song

In my sixty-seventh year I am prisoner
of the whites. Between the spaces
of barred metal, my people, my dead
people, appear, sullen as judges.

Sun Fish is gone. Thunder is gone.
Nea-a-pope is gone. White Beaver is gone.
Wa-pel-lo is gone. Quash-qua-me is gone.
Ma-ta-tah is gone. Gomo is gone.
Wash-e-own is gone. Singing Bird is gone.
Wa-co-me is gone. Ra-she-pa-ho is gone.
Mu-ka-ta-quet is gone. Ma-she-na is gone.

The arrow of execution, the waiting
arrow of death, the goose-quilled
scratching shaft of black blood
is taking the lands east of the

Kishwaukee, is taking the lands
between the Rock and the Great
River, is taking all Indian lands,
is taking all wild game. Our

brother buffalo is gone.
Bear and deer refuse to shake
newborn from their bellypouch.
No thing escapes the white man's

guns. And the coming arrow
is opening its raven teeth and
bending the weight my dying
skin wrinkles before it.

Ottawa are dying.
Chippewa are dying. Potawatomi are dying.
Fox and Winnebago are dying.
Sioux are dying. Menominee are dying.
Cree and Kickapoo are dying.
Oto are dying. Iowa are dying.
Osage and Cherokee are dying.

Delaware and Muscow are dying.
Omaha and Quapaw are dying.
Ponca are dying. Kansa are dying.
Sauk are dying.

The white blade is stroking
flesh of all Indian peoples.
In the blue marsh our bones
twitch and thrash their invisible

flesh. Molds of arm and leg
become rock and press into
limestone paths on journeys
deeper along the way our

leading, rigid tracks bring us.
We are the color of earth clay.
Our spirits have shown us how to
shape soil in holy image.

Clear streams run in our veins.
Pure air wings our bodies home.
Our sorrow for lost lands
and lost people is the sorrow

of spirits, the sorrow of our fathers,
earth sorrow. Our lives are rising
in wings of smoke from bone
fires on mountainsides into

the shuddering black torch of sky,
into flaming night,
into dreams and song.

Ceremony

The ringing of the night
was still in my eyes
when I went out that tenth
or eleventh summer
of my years. The ground
began to open among the wood
land shadows

and the birds webbed
me in song until a rustling
on a bushy hill where the sun
was born and all else died.
To share a mystic brotherhood
with the sun I would seek
a transformation, the spitting

of unholy blood and the waking.
The windsheet of my father's words
stood stern as warriors,
"To tear the wall of darkness
down and find the hidden
man and subdue him
you must risk everything,

you must bare your chest
and as the sharpness
of the blade touches you
like a feather, kill your
enemy, make him your friend."
Blades of sunlight jabbed
my neckskin and I shivered in damp

knowledge. I parted my eye
lids, saw the path to follow and set
off softly thumping the pitched ground.
A border of stones
pressed heavy my thoughts.
A small bow, five arrows
and the wise hand of the earth

spirit nimbly moved with my body.
A snake snapping ropelike
threw its skin. Wetborn, it
unraveled toward a briarbush
as its hollow sheath fluttered
away in the wind.
My head, fuzzled

with noonday heat,
scattered the clouds that bobbed
the surface of a steam.
Hung bellyflat into the water
I saw the dead eyes of my head
shatter as waterbugs swam
through the mouth of my other mouth.

A leaf pocketed just below
the surface floated past. Suddenly down
stream within easy reach of my eyes
a deer was drinking.
Fearful that my reflection
would carry to the deer, I
faded, back strung like a bow,

into woods. Mossfooted
and timbered tight as a tree I moved
slowly forward. An arrow
wrapped its fingers around my
bowstring and as my arm bent
back like a sapling caught
on hooks of the wind,

the deer gently turned
its head and shot
its eyes into mine.
The fluid brown were my mother's
eyes, tufted, pillowy cattails
and wide staring. In her eyes
I saw my face and as I touched

the skin of my mother's brown
warm breast with my flopping wet mouth,
her black hair fell on my cheek like rain.
Caught on the arrow of time I could
not move or quiet the drums in my chest.
The deer came two searching steps
closer and like a contented fawn dropped

to its knees, eyes lapping
mine. As in a dream, from far
away I saw my fingers slide
down from my bow and an arrow gentle
as a flaxball float out
to drive itself into my mother's smiling face,
and as it pitched forward spilling

red liquid like a too sweet plum
on my feet, I fell
down the shaft of my throat
into my coiling stomach. The deer
shivered as with a chill then
stretched taut. A small bubbling
stream wound snakelike from the deer's

mouth into the clear spooling stream.
I gutted the deer and swinging
its still warm body to my back
its head tucked on my shoulder
as if whispering into my ear
I started toward Saukenuk.
Our eyes gleamed bright.

A red trail tracked us against
the sun scampering in the low
branches of the forest. Near
the time when the night
begins climbing out from treeshadows
two wolves caught our scent.
Yapping, blood smell on their

tongues they paused nearby
on a rock outcropping. I laid
the deer down and swiftly whistled
two arrows into one wolf and as the other
jumped, sailing at me, an arrow
eclipsed it midair, joined like a fifth
leg, and flashing knives embraced

my arm. An arrow alive in my hand
thrust a single tooth into the wolf's head and once
again it bit into the fur, my hands
violently shaping and molding, and it relaxed
and lay like a sleeping dog
in my arms. Sweat, not tears
shut my eyes down hard
and bloodsalt, the sacred ceremonial

blood was in my mouth.
A little farther on, above
the treetops I could see
the campfires of my village
curling white smoke high into the sky.
I felt no weight in the body
of the dead child in my arms
which I would soon lay at my father's feet.

First Battle

Down where the Pecatonica breaks
its anklebone and riverspray whiffs
like snow unsettled my first

battle was fought. Our band of thirty
braves came upon the Osage who stole
game from our land and murdered our people.

Warring cries and death yells fell
from our tongues as we fell
upon them. A beak-nosed warrior

of my father's age sent his spear
toward me but mine found him first,
the spearpoint buckling skin,

bending its impression inward,
the shift of weight lifting from
the solid finger's probed entry,

hot blood bursting its salt,
a firespray in motion of fire
at the unknown end of heat

where no man returns to speak.
Searing, bone cocked open entry,
the warm expanding cavern brings

home its dead like silent children.
Uncontrolling birthpains see
the brief connection, pull apart

the living strands and lose space
in space. A shudder passes its final
breath. My arms, shaking with a new

9

energy, upravel the escaping power.
Alone in final moments that no
man can share except with those

before him and that sharing
is much deeper, is of the blood
lost from a mother's bellowing

thighs at the instant of coming
life or death when the hollow
cavity fills with the air

of light and presses its second
head to cool morning pain
that is no pain and the warrior

or new child is peeled from
a transparent skin, the skin some
day it will again take up and place

its last cry of breath into.
That which has once contained
what it has come to call the same

reflection from either side, never
severs the connecting cord, only turns
and turns and turning finds the risk

that grows a body. Unable to use
the passion we approach with heads
in the center of eyes that see

what they cannot, we place the terrifying
mask of ourselves in our blind steps
and follow the motherly dark glow

of other bodies. My father twisting
on the end of my spear
the naked mist of our enemies

found his son awakening a man.
In that awakening my mother's
brief sweat flooded my skin,

the prickly wind sucking
at moisture collecting like scalps
that disappear in turning light.

Mother, in the cradle of your empty
belly unloose my brothers and sisters,
Mother carry the seed the spear

my father leaves, in conceiving agony
mother, O pure mother keep
our joining fiber hidden, safe.

Song of Justice

One of my brave sons
captured by some white men
had escaped and returned home
closer to death than life.
As he told us, he was taken

to their camp and hung upside
down, his hair cut off and thick
grease poured over his body. He
was then covered with feathers.
The lids of his eyes were cut off,

stakes shoved into his nose slits,
his arms bound tightly with leather
cords and small cuts made into
his wrists and hands so that
the slow fall of blood would bring

much pain. He was loosened
and only because of strong
will kept his breath to here.
The man of healing came to cure
his wounds and bind his eyes

while all the men gathered in
council lodge to speak of this.
The holy fires were lit.

Hear me, O my braves.
This deed will not go unpunished.

O strong warriors lift your spears,
lift your bows, gather your arrows,
O people of peace we must speak
to the heavens for justice. Arise,
O songs of vengeance, sing words

of power, sing for clear vision your children.
We must turn the earth under their feet
and hang trees from their legs like night bats.
The heaving air, the collapsing air will leave
their lungs and fall in brittle leaves.

Slick blood, greasy blood, bright as eyes
will cover their bodies in sweat
and our hands pluck skin like red
fruit and crawl their flesh as flies,
crawl flesh as spiders, crawl

flesh as fleaticks, crawl flesh
as crablice and the caw, caw, caw
of their screams become sky fire
spilling from coiled tongues. All skin
removed, the feathers red with their

blood will cry for freedom, for flight,
and we will give them the flight of a
fieldmouse wrenched in the toe claws
of hawkbirds, tearing for their bubbly
fat flesh and it will rot in our jaws.

Their eyes will roll with blind stones
in the bloodlight of sun and unable
to rip those sleepless, flaming eyes
a new vision will open to them. Their
unstopping sight seethe in the pain

of what they have seen. Our faces
will be dreams that live in them like worms.
Our arms will reach into their noses
and pull the air out and pull the blood
from their skin and unknot the liquid guts

that tangle and weave like snakes. Our
women and children will wrap teeth
around white arms and the soft bones snap.
We will open new lungs in their arms and breathy
red, scorching red, exhale its life into our

open hands. And they crawl from the village
of death. They will be animals with no name
and the pain in their bodies cry sick, hot heavens.
O people arise, harvest the bowels
of our enemies, the sharp blade is coming,

the torches smash their light,
we go to seek power in the warm belly of death.

In the Arms of Snake

The moment my father dyed
my anklebone color to the scarlet
of sunset as the sun drags its wounded
sky into cleansing, I felt the mooncut
of knife fangs bite deeper than the

rattlesnake blade. Quailgrass boiled, winding
like a forest of snakes, crawled their shadows
over my face skin. The pain wrapping my
leg, coiling, tightened, tightened. The movement
of stone, weighted limbs, dead branches of black

oak grew in my veins, in the violent
flushing scales of my awakened leg.
And my father digging, scooping, planting
the slim throat of his knife into my skin,
searching for the dark root from where

all men descend into the flesh of their
children. The air bursting from my lungs
like snakes escaping birth shells, bright airy
fear biting my eyes, toothless, raw.
The rigid, worn-down shine of rising blades,

my leg unclasping its hip, severs
the red joining fibers and like a blind,
eyeless worm, flops, flops, thrashes
into black. The thick, unclosing eyelids
shed surface. Like a river of snakes

my vision ravels in my skull, flows
into the cracks of familiar bone.
My father, now a knife, cannot stop his plunge,
and all my breaking strips reel away
with life. My fingers and toes ribbon

like garter snakes. My arms, bullsnakes
or timber rattlers, shaking their child's
toys and bending, parting the stalks,
reeds jab in the ground. The pure, sharp
form of my body bites into the earth,

spitting my poison, my juice into
the sucking, quivering, dying, red-eyed
emptiness. The heat of fever has cooled.
Sweat drains its venom.
The earth relaxes in my arms, slumps

its weight and falls. In the silent
hollows under my skin, snake eggs
are budding, stemming, hatching their
twisted, snaky petals. My veins move
on their own, blue, and tightening

their coils to invisible bones.
Horny tails switch in my belly.
The snouts of my fingers blotch,
upturn, stripe along the sides.
My jaws, my hooked teeth, expand

under this flickering tongue. Vipers
hiss in my nose. Logs and leaves
drift mounds around me. Tangles
of my flesh stretch for sunny rocks.
My glands swell, the liquid drips

and spurts, I cannot contain it and striking
my father's leg I suck and suck, the joyous
serpent bleeding the salt, sucking
and spitting and sucking the blood
of my father, my womb.

Coming Home

Awake, I see the forest
go about its chores.
In the dawn each grass stalk

is burning its dew
and yellowjackets inspect
sunburnt clover faces.

Birch shadows roll out and lie
in neat rows. Crickets shrill
as wheezing children saw

their stickly legs together. A willow
shakes two sparrows from her hair
and squatting next to her a dwarf

oak hides his deformed legs.
In the delicate breeze raging
cornflowers flutter like butterflies.

I haul up straight my bark
smooth trunk and see that
chigger tracks necklace my waist.

Black burrs hook their long
teeth to my legs.
Not sure that if I stay

this new family would accept
my strange ways I decide
to return to my people.

The drone of memory,
of village sounds and dayward
gaze will not yet surrender

me to the forest.
Moonseed nettle mutters
in my ears, but I

cannot return the speech,
the language I have not learned.
Tunneled badger fashion

into my silent burrow for
how many days has lifted
dead skin from my eyes

and now bursting as milk
weed pods my arms shed
their shaggy log shells.

Baby's breath pause on peeled
stems and do not ruffle
their toes at my passing.

Cattails flare up like fluffy torches.
The reborn world takes me in
a warm flat palm and a haycock wind

pats my spreading cheeks.
The days ahead part their budding
branches then wrap around each other,

trailing arms behind my fading
form like lost brothers.
I come home.

Death of Lost Singing

Under the dull blade
of summer our crops are dying.
Pinched stalks drain all color.
Pods shrivel in dry age. Roots
gag on their own choking, sucking

throat tubes, pulling and sucking
in final gasps at the moisture no
longer there. Great scabs of ground
crack apart in island fields and curl
at the flaked edge of their bruises.

Swarms of shimmering brown dust
sizz and chittle in powdery heaps
in the breathing caves of our
shrinking ears. Alone in each
man's slowing blood the shine

of red gloamed liquid pings
as it disappears in air. The great
mouth of earth splits in all directions.
Forest trails widen into rivers
that clog and choke their sand.

Straining for dreams of water
our fires do not sleep. Our village
festers like a sore. Into the sunken
belly of winter this winter, into
the shrunk mouth of our stomachs

we will put horsemeat and flesh
of decayed animals and then tree roots
and dogfur. Finally the gnawing
pains will go beyond pain to mean
we have turned our sides in

and the eating away of ourselves
has begun. For two or three
moons our limbs will hang
like splintered branches and the blinking
mouths we carry reskin themselves

like wounds under the sun's
cold lance. The shuffling twigs
our toebones become drop off.
We pass them through flames
and eat. The children, O the sad

children lose their doll stuffing
and rip at skin they can reach
with jaws they cannot clench.
Our women we do not recognize.
Our eyes fail to see

or shut down their vision
at the dark walls they must
pass through. The black glow
of our skin is like fishbones
in the stone huts of frozen rivers.

Snow piles its corpses at
the door our life is opening.
Many of my people will not feel
the humming blow gently lift
them to those final drifts.

Huddled in dark corners of their
lodges, teeth rattling like wind,
others will know where their brothers
go in silent rising as they pass through
the opening bright, unclosing mouth.

Their shadows too weak to follow
will remain and in the slow
devouring light of hunger, eat
and eat and eat
their ripe, lovely black.

O father wind send your rains
of pity to my starving people.
O mother lay your great shield
of sun to rest. Cry your children.

Flight

Over the branches of plum and apple
rivers, past the Prophet's village
and toward the Great River's yellow
banks my people made their flight.
In the night air, pale arrow

moon shafts whitened backs dead
weighted with hide sacks. The slow
movement of forest dreams risen
in shadow shine rustled dark
trees. Fires of eyes burned in vast

passing rushlight. Sailing leafy
currents batted their popples. Across
the ground, shadow rolled on shadow.
Searching the forward path all eyes
detached their sockets and scuttled

into distance. Harsh leather scent, woodrot
and loam musk mix their breaths. The tik,
tik, tik, tik of a coot pecks the silence.
The separate skin of an animal running
from our snapping form keeps up

the hip and slide, images stick to what
brush them. The hew of moonlight
slices our shadow skin. Again breaking
off in hedgehog scurry an animal drags
the clacking wood vines. His blunt

run shares our sight, the fleeing whisk
from danger to the danger we cannot
escape. Helpless in the path that always
tracks us, just to the left from corners
of our eye in the swift flurry

of a blink, it is there. Always
waiting for exhaustion to fold its
final blanket over our beating noses
and the round approach of its full
light beyond the sight of inner

vision, empty in the heavy curve
our hands make in protection.
Lifting the jagged prints our feet
slap the ground in frenzy of new
fear. Nightshapes enlarge our flat

bodies. Through the damp gully grass
we spin our fright. Among my people,
women and children clutch hands like gravestones.
The furrow of a stream pulls at its riffles.
We cross where shale stones ridge

a smooth pool. Drinking where an iced drivel
brings new blood from under rock our gaunt
whispers float like spirits, colorless as breathing.
I know the way. Ke-o-kuck among my braves
is unsure our direction is near enough

the blue mounds of the Rock, our home lands.
The active force of pressing on arouses
my shape of bones and drawing life from watery
moss graze we rise again and come
to our intent. A horned owl grums his wail.

Halfway up a hill the clear path shuts down
around us. Briarthorns lash their fangs in
thickening bushes. Gusts of imagined cries
sweep our legs. Hairy fingers tangle hair.
Unable to stand straight the leading men

twist deeper in reckless pain. The strip
of ground closes us, thins the flat roll
where we had come. Shifting, swirling,
the changing wall of forest blows dense
the valley our faces become. Caught

in a hawk's nest our bodies become one
with the awkward loss of feeling. Holding
my hand between the whipping haze
I move to the left, to the direction
my death takes, toward the sure knowledge

and a path opens. The hatchet arms of branches
fall away and I am in the eye
a clearing holds up to the moon's stare.
My people have not followed and turning
uncertain on hard earth I sink heavy

with sounds descending in rushes
of dark wings and slashes of air
tearing their clear welts and arrow
tipped light piercing skin.
My cries throw hooks into the dark

life I had left. The false shadow
releases itself. Under the pressure
my legs cast, the sinking ground melts.
Beating wings lifting, beating, bearing up
the light shell I do not recognize

I free even this body. Rising, I become
the howling sun and length of vision
stretches the lined horizon. No root
attaches its clasp. The waving trees turn
to grass. Rivers unloop their veins.

Eagles grow dizzy with height.
Rising, I go beyond myself.
Still lifting, the sky below drops
its skin. The shrill hiss of speed
darkens its whine into a great sigh.

The black flame opens a side in clean
simple cold. The deep night takes me in.
From far below the jarring cry
of my people flutters its faint wings.
I know I cannot stop the words

my blood speaks and feel the slow
return of wind to my chest, the gentle
insect buzz of stunned thoughts.
The smoky air draws back to fire.
From where I fall the rising hill

becomes dawn. My woman pours water
into me. In warm patches my people sleep.
The still beauty of morning rests
a dewy hand. In swelling daylight
the paths will lie straight before us.

The far country, the full lands
we go to open in friendship.
In clear, sure sound, they call our names.

Early Life

My young puppy face
in the days of my father's
lodge knew much happiness.

The habits of my people,
laws and customs sit stiff
as stone watchtowers. No

death song is on their lips.
The medicine feast carries
on its back food and pelts

to our dead people. A young
brave becomes a flame in crane
dance for a wife. With fire he

enters the lodge of chosen
woman and waits for her dark
tongue to fold the blinking light,

smother, accepting wish. Headhung
on his waist my father's bag
of sweetgrass braid, cedar leaves,

hawk tailfeathers and buffalo tooth
would become my son. My ways
of deadfall and rope snare traps,

bow-drill firemaking, beaming
and fleshing a hide, weaving
basswood bark, ribbing a canoe

and arrow fletching filled
the learning days. From the mighty
water straining at its banks

to the sloping shouldered bluff
behind our village I grew wise
to beaver, mink and deer, rabbit,

porcupine and the whispered
forest speech. Descending,
the beautiful woman from

clouds shared venison
and through the spread veins
of her right hand brings

forth corn and beans. Through
knee-high corn the coming stones
rear up on notches of axe

and spears. Dried fish
and bark-rice mats fit the flat
walls of winter lodges. Quillwork

tangles their reedy fingers.
Cradleboards wear the bound
backs of babies. Plaited tumplines

shake loose their fibered coils.
The spiral of the uncurling
snowsnake was my favorite game

and its tapered shuttling arch
scorched like starfall. My
bone whistle, laughing from the horned

spoon of a mountain peak, became
thunder and magic. My father
sheds the water of his body now,

and taking up the skin of wolf
or deer scratches thigh skin, the raw
blood gorging hooked arrows.

The wrong dream wins his breathing
and a streaked face, oil-plated skin
drinks color from his blood. Otter

skin replaces each leg in outward
sweep of covered stalking shaft.
Hickory bow, black locust, the brittle

cane arrows support the weighted points.
Awaken father. Awaken. Open the sky
of your eyes. Draw back your head

before the soft fall of Cherokee
axes. Their falling hands already
lie upon your skull and into it

my pain. O hunter, inhuman
bare-necked wounded dance.
O dying father who
cannot share your children's pain.

The Offering

Come to where the black
bear has left his claws
in the skins of walnut

and sluiceberry, over the foot
hills' tawn breasts, to this
slender underpart of the fall

sky, we bring our gifts.
Our wandering smoke carries up
its black tips of prairie color.

To the far land where the moon
sleeps, to forests of clear water
and proud animals to our final

home we ascend in the arms
of our smoke, in our waiting
hands white-tailed deer, wild

fruit, river otter, pond turtles,
rabbit, walleye, rock bass,
woodcocks, painted pheasant, heron

eggs, stone dove, smooth shells
of corn and beans, in the easy
smoke wingbeat we lose our ground.

The wide blue eye of the sky
has seen us bending
in a sacred ring and the heads

of groundstones rise to meet us.
The swift heart of all people,
the Kickapoo, Potawatomi, Huron,

Iowa and Sauk join their beating
breath to the blood of earth.
Arise feathery smoke, leap

gifts, back to your brothers.
In our assembled birth keep
within your great womb of sun

the breath that comes through
our life. Burn. Burn the sickness
from our limbs, burn our weak

eyes in the light we cannot see.
In the heat of blooming fire
flowers brush away your enemies.

Blaze in favor your people
like thick bushes, our children
heavy and firm fruit, place

your feet in our feet to guide
our steps. In your bright arms
our arms are burning. No weight

is in us. We soar on broad
wings. In a private sight
the pure smoke lifts eyes.

Height has left our bodies.
In empty air we are all
movement and we feel you move

in us. Shucks of skin
fall away, fall from still
burning bodies long below.

Into the calm face all
time brings her children.
Horse hoofs echo their last

calls to us. Each spirit
is content in the light,
smooth journey's sound. Blue

burning light exhausts its smoke.
The single flame wraps us
like new children. The white

flow leaves, burnt, and in
pure beauty we stream back
to meet our life growing

in holy branches of trees
that take form in coming
passion. The simple, silent order.

First Meeting

When we had set the pain
of bearing death to our right
side, tending silver-birched

canoes as we tend our children,
the unknown men came to us.
My people scattered like silent foxes

at the first unfamiliar growl
of their tongues, but in my
upheld hand was sun

between our coming peoples,
and in their speech a windy heat
that spoke to us of tribes

beyond our home rivers, past
the lands of Fox and Sioux
who had mingled their bloods

in friendship with the peace of brothers.
My people follow only the touch
our fathers place upon us with no

sacred mouth speaking doubt,
with no division of war
in our thoughts we offered

the blood of our wrists
to white blood to join
us as one in peace.

The holy pipes were lit and the ascending
smoke was pure as dove feathers.
An eagle shadow crossing

on the ground was good sign
and so a meal was held
with stalks of maize, rich deer

meat, fish and cock flesh,
sweet rabbit and wild fruits offered
to our tallow-skinned friends.

Rubbing its spiked chaff over
and over the lumped skin
in my throat, fear rose

and fell back, then again
rising to the last reach
of my vision trembled in

a swelling frothy cry, the last
cry of a dying child
as its talons rip at the full

bellyskin, rip the round empty
cave wall of its devouring self.
Spilling to the ground my dancing

dying children tore teeth
on their own flesh and like a mad
wolfpack panted the ground

with foul blood. Alive in the dream
that my shadow drags behind me
I could not act in knowledge.

My stone arms and legs red
in the bright shine of escaping
pain were mountains aching

in their cold roots. Above the flying
spun flurry, white crows calm
as groundspring pools made their slow

flight, breathing my peoples' upward draft.
Like wolf fangs my eyes sunk
into gourded cheeks, rattling jaws

of teeth slit their blades
into my head from all sides
and beginning to give flight

to a scream my fear returned in hand.
An acorn skull burst under clasped fingers.
My senses returned. I was aware

of gifts the white men were giving
my people. Laughter was snow
flakes to our campfires. The future

frozen in my throat I felt, but could not see.
A smiling, drunken corpse, I could not see.

Forest Vision

All morning the grey sky
has pressed its rainy finger
tips into my hut's roof.

For two days my heart
has sent its roots deep
into the ground and held

me in a strange body
here on this spot. Now
the air is quiet and my

spirit is quietly drawing
up woodish earthen claws.
Released of what a man alone

will come to call his own
full bloody breath, the appearance
shakes a wing like a windy branch

and always the vision of the bird,
untouched in smooth flight,
has folded me in the inner

descent of our familiar journey.
The circling hawk has fixed
its one black eye to the heaving

frown of movement my body
makes through the slick forest.
Unable to know why I go

this way I watch the bouncing
green-headed wild grapes. Strands
of spider traps wrap their thin

nooses to my neck. An owl
inquires of my progress and everything
seems bending to a purpose.

At the bottom of a cedar valley
the copper-skinned arm of a stream
slides into thick briars. Footprints

in soft mud enter the stream
and I cannot tell how long
they lost the foot that placed them.

The substance of the earth
does not betray the print
of someone's undisturbing

pass and like the surface
of this stream, what a man leaves
behind was there before,

the ground is the mark and proof
only of itself.
A thorny bush lunges at my hand

and leaves a fading white-scarred vein.
Dragging a ripped smoky blanket over
its head the sun again sends

grizzled tears upon me. In no mood
for wonder I make for the shelter
of an oak overhang. Looking back

at the ponds my feet make
I see the simple cycle fill
with its own action. Soon the steam

of night will sweep me in
her raging breath and cushy
steps follow to my people.

My rising eyes will show
the path we have lost.
Weep no more O my sad people,
the sky will share our sorrow.

Morning Village

In the opening air
sag-plum branches rung
the hill's flowering pouch

and the sun flitching through
robin and jay nests is like a fox
squirrel's scamper. Pit-a-pit,

pit-a-pit a skree bird chitters.
Peachberry and rosecups, pale and sun
shoots whiffle their cool scents.

At the fires' edge hornback
stones stack their heads. Twigs
hawker skeletal fingers in switch rushes.

A slobbering elm saps his pocked
crust. Children suddenly appear,
pinched in sleepy crabwalk, then

like dogs wild with fleas roll,
dirt flaking their brownness.
A rooster gaggles, shivers his saggy

chin and trots off. Chowling
in angry violence a baby flares
up from the river. Powpa-cha,

powpa-cha, powpa-cha an old
woman thumps wheat powder
with a jack bone. Grain-meal leaves

flip at the ends and hocks of maize
bare their teeth. My village
opens its brilliant eye.

The light of the hive
sound stares me flat
in the face. In my eyes

a boy is coming forward
from his dead mother's reach
of shadow and to his light

breath my hand takes up
its air of movement. His
flax floe fingered touch.

So gentle. A puff of sad
lips that expect a mewl
to pad forth. A timid fawn

face uprooted, waxed beyond
its glimmering birth spore.
The feel of more than

my arms can hold
in weight has slowed my steps
of thought. Why, my son

seems to say to the boy
in myself, in all my
lost children. Why, he speaks

with no question in his word.
Why, he calls from his spinning
web. Why, his melting shadow

pools my feet. From a sacred
secret depth the word is stern
as a father. My people see only

the ground they stand upon, I say.
A final whisper, he smiles, and yes
the winds hiss yes, yes, yes.

Battle of Sink Hole

My band of braves and I,
having avenged the death
of a murdered friend, were attacked

under the stone nose of bluffs
at the Great River. We ran
into timbered bushes and like

the first tree falling in a storm
I killed the lead white man.
Before we could prepare ourselves

again, they surrounded us and drove
us back to the edge of a deep sink
hole. We began digging holes for

protection and as we waited the attack,
the circling ascent of death
song made its wingless flight.

I heard the whites talking
and their chopping words
spoke to me of fear. Standing in my

pit of open grave, half in the earth,
the killing dusk settled on our shoulders.
Beneath the lower surface of where

I lay the ground slowly pulled
back, away and down, damp as
birthskin and forming feet and legs

in my reflection. Plant roots,
sinewed and taut, snapped their strength.
A scale of dirt unthreaded its suck

and rolled over me. Oozing through
my feet, skull fluid crooked the wavy
channels my toes dug. Like the slow

earth-curved inhalation of this soiled
giant lung, the intake drew me in.
The peace that goes beyond despair

took my eyes and my body skew
deepened its fastened, hanging free
death. My ebbing flesh gave to

the pull. The lid of night shut
back its nickering stars. Away
in the leafy forest patter

I heard my final cry,
the last note of death song
streaking in downward plunge.

The end's upright boundary
endures the purpose of both
sides, I seem to say to my

unhooking bones. In traveling night
the closeness of my father's
smile takes up moonteeth. What

dogpath rises to my knees? I cannot
pass the flesh-bearing chief hide
to my worms. O father, rise

my strong hand, shake the limbs
of your men with life. Tear
back the dark farther. Striding

from my burial I aroused my
braves and quivering forth like arrows
we made our attack. In the dead

air only we were alive.
The white men had gone. The moon
was rising like a question.

Alone in my sky I felt the answering
black. In flaming hawk-black wrist
blood the straight-edged answer

back and forth began to move
and move and move.

Swimming in the Rock

Emptying my body of its last breath
I am free to walk the paths
of rivers at such depths

that mucky bottom sand sucking
on my hollow, moving steps
cannot keep up. Crawfish and finger

leeches kiss my flesh and wet
red pores pass their salt. Floating
its gold dome the bobbing sky takes the shape

of my eyes. I pull the riffling
surface on my head
and I break skin like a bone.

My birdwing lungs flap in new
air and currents press their spilling
noses to me. I like the feel of living

in two worlds. Below my floating belly
my legs remove themselves. Like fat
driftwood I watch them go and am alone

in the air. Riverwater becomes
my blood, it eddies in curved veins.
A soft dead fish rolls his bloating

body into mine. I am unable to take
my eyes from his, his pregnant soft
wild eyes. He wraps around my chest

and floats off. In the air above
someone is breaking branches and slinging
the ripped arms into the water.

Along the shore I see the rocks
putting on moss. The green robes
are three shades brighter under river.

Like motherbirds with worms in their beaks,
my legs are coming back. There is no
ceremony, they just clamp onto my hips

and swivel footfins into a cloud
whorl and the liquid twang
of my ascending body frees the river.

Dream

The waxy night air whirs
in my footsteps like tree locusts.
Nightbirds skittle upward shadow
movements and flowing over
the wounded meadowgrass

my limp arms stretch toward the ground.
Peacock lily and rose jimp
joggle foolish heads. I shed
a breath and feel the world
lift out of my ears. Entering

dead flesh I become alive.
A right hand holds my fingers
in its shallow grave and spider
prints hitch their empty paws together.
A sweet froth is ripening like plums

on my lips as I pitch
into the opening air of a new form.
I don't know what I bring
from my familiar bones, these dizzy
steps do not move with me. Eyeballs daggle

in black holes then rear up on roots ends
at the sting of moonlight.
Scrabbling on the ground my people
do not recognize their chief. Pecking
corn they do not turn to see

me turn toward the path
the sun will not take. Alone
in its forest an old body calls
its name. Drifting leaves pile their flat feet
at my feet. Clinks of sunlight rattle

in the treetops. Deep in my home
earth I rise up like a dawn.
All is quiet. Awake in my dreams
I cast down whole days. Rolling on
its side a she bear is dying.

She answers my baying, moaning,
and our search for reason
in the pain of dreams binds
the cord of solitary flesh.
A mother bear, and I the child

she could not find to deliver
forth the only message of flesh
that moved in her mountains of night.
The vast, unearthed stench
plunges from her coming light

in the half-light of trembling air.
Her dusky fur splits at touch
and lifting my sleeping spirit
she carries me to her cave
and my silver tears become sleeping

Dream

children on the slide of cheek,
the bitter gash, the blue loon's hollow nest,
the naked prowl of my days
fills with the coming light.
From my blind eyes it is coming.

Buffalo Hunt

It is the open spaces
we most fear, white as cloud
banks with no recess
to secret our untouched
hands and so it was

the day of the great buffalo
kill. High hid on a spruce-lopped
hill, bold into my middle years
I came upon the place of the god's
spine which overgaped a garland

fitted grassland plain. Six white men
framed a herd of thirty buffalo,
and with a flush of thundered smoke
began to kill them. A deathly motion
of my eyes was all that was alive

in me, a stone body anchored
to the hilltop above the flutter
of last cries. In the dying fog
day I felt witness to the murder
of a family, the passing of a tribe.

Before the noon sun turned its back
the white men were gone and the slumbered
herd puddled in their shade.
I made my way to the fields
and my quickened heart rammed

Buffalo Hunt

the cliffs of my chest. Two buffalo
were carved of meat, twelve skinned
and the others red with dead blood.
Thick moist meat soon rotting
would cover hunter's glory in fly swarms.

A force of inborn sickness clutched
my legs and stiff in clumps
of grazing flesh I became my huddled
tribe and all around us
decaying sullen horses and on them

banded forms of men and empty
eyes were stones and in the smoked
curled sky, a hooved
pounding descended on my people
and our stamping breath was blood

and the red mist of scalding cries rose
in flocks and suns from all
directions floated on the wind
to us, floated to our center
and as our fingers reached out

to shield or touch we flamed,
light, a hallow rising of glazed
images and liquid forms became air
and becoming air we died
and gave up our flesh and skins

and our tears became rain,
our cries became wind.
My gaze returned.
Understanding there was nothing
I might do I set off toward my village.

Troubled with my bruised thoughts,
I could hear only the echoes
of my next footfall. A butterfly brushed
my cheek, wings folded,
and my feet felt the ground's turning face.

Away in the distance I saw
the smoke of my people. This night
they would be cooking rabbits.
Soon, O lost brothers, we will leave
for new lands.

Battle Dance

A chant has taken the night
upon its shoulders and carried
her kicking black mask
to our village. Our fires'

eyes see the omen of war
and it twists into the sky
with chanting. Children with mothers
deep in shadows feel the fires'

brazed fingers on their face
and the chant swirls like a birdswarm
into the opening sky, into the broken
dawn, on the feathers of holy wings,

from the blackmarsh, from the stone forest,
from our father's ground swell, into an
opening mouth, past the river's jagged teeth,
to the arms of death, to the land of shadows,

to the light, to the light of eyes
to the light of our skin
to the light of our blood
to our brothers

to our brothers dead,
to our brothers dead.
The drum has felt a quickening
in its chest and from a distance

an echo repeats the moaning landscape.
In the new sky the moon's pale
echo tilts its thumb tips
and rolls a skullish smile.

A brightening wind stirs the slumbered
embers and pulls salt juice from the cornered
mouths of men. Clay red, plant
green tendrils, bark brown streak

each face. A pulsed heart
becomes the rythmic pounding.
The spirits of spirits rattle
in the firelight. Flames wail

in the heat of naked flesh.
Animal bones clock, clock, clock
as the dancing becomes skeletal.
Past the flying grave

black image, past the morning's
hoary cry, into the arms of death
we send our singing
arrow, into the wombs

of white women, into the white
children in those wombs, into
the white men in those children.
O sacred arrow, O sacred singing arrow

fly fast from our unafraid arms,
fly fast to our enemy.
Bring to your people dancing
dead heads and naked red

eyes plucked like berries,
and bring us tongues laughing
like children and arms flapping
for air and the gold hair

of women for our women.
We will drink the white man's
blood and our skin will burn
redder and dead flesh

nourish our crops. Corn will grow
with rows of eyes and wheat
crawl up in hands and our people
be strong in the days of our fathers.

2.

Up the Rock River
to a sandbar with its
yellow belly up like a dead

fish my warriors came. We
went into the forest and soon
came to the white men's camp.

With skirling yells and our knives
turning in hands we fell
on the whites and killed them all.

Twenty-two whites died and no
brave of mine was lost.
On returning to our village

a great feast was begun.
I as chief was happiest among
my people, I as chief alone

felt the empty coming days
in my heart and saw the
flat smiling faces of my people

dead in the ground at my feet.
From across the great waters
more white people would come.

More white people would die
but with them so would many among
my people. The Sioux, the Potawatomi,

the Fox, the Chippewa, all friends,
all enemies would be cast up
into the air and the white wind

from the east sweep all
Indian people to lands of the dead.
My thorn of sorrow was lost

in my people's happiness,
and I wept not knowing
from where my tears came.

Singing Bird

Treebats would disappear
into the dark caves of your hair
and their bleeking
bleeking cries ring from a wooden

distance. A hollowness
raises its arms in my throat
and gently lifts my mouth up
from your orange petal lips.

The snow feathered softness of your face
is a new wildness to me.
The first time, I was frightened
at your sudden stiffening when you

reared back and flopping like a fish
out of water were strange to me.
Later my lungs puffed out like bushes
when you told me it was only

your love dance on my finger
tips. Elderberry and baskets
of fruit flowers grow somewhere
in your brown skin for in all truth

when my tongue enters the taste
and scent of you, wild fields
and untouched meadowlands open
their bright thighs to me.

When I am gone, I make
the shadow following me your shadow
and when I lie down in the furry
brightness of moon, a tufted buffalo

blanket becomes your rabbit-warm flesh.
The bounding elk lifting high into the branches
of the winter wind across a frozen snow lake
is no beauty when your cool milky

shoulders sink into my lips.
The liquid fluttering stars
in the silent waters of a willow pond
are your eyes. Sometimes at night

to see your sleeping arms and legs
vine my blind limbs I feel
a savage animal lashing and tearing
at my breastkin from within

my chest and I tremble in your strength
and arch the arrow of my body
flashing into the teeth
of the wind, flashing into the deep

black sky, flashing outward into
the holy grave of your womanhood.

Death's Path

Hearing that my people
had been attacked at the joining
of two rivers I made great haste
to come to this place.
On a small island deftly snagged

at the sloping rock rapids I found
my people scattered as on
a hail-plundered ground. All
was silent except for the chittering
of locusts. Among the dead were twelve

of my bravest warriors, seven of our women
and five children not yet old enough
to hold a knife. The children's arms
were bent like knuckled hands and the
moonpale head of an unborn child

hung ripped from its mother's
pouched belly. Wormwood eyes
glared defiant at the unblinking sun
and each skin moved as if alive
with maggot flesh. One maiden

pure as morning dew held in her hand
her loamy, blood-brown tongue torn
from death's naked laugh. The brother
of my wife caught in my throat
a heaving and I swacked

away the blood ticks that were furrowing
into his frozen eyeballs as if searching
for the truth a man gives up, the truth
a man gains in such a dying.
Lifting my arms to the heavens

I cried out, flinging swollen
tears on the mettled ground. A
wind wet with riverspray combed
the wailing hair of willow weeds.
I fell silent to my knees

and prayed with all my power as chief
that my vengeance of justice would sweep
like an earth-soaked whirlwind
to those who had murdered my people.
Never again to know the peace

of my village or the silent friendship
of our forests I will be the blade
on the neck of the white man,
and each slash will be my lost braves
and each cry will be for my crying women
and each drop of blood my spilling, dying children.

Defeat at Bad Axe

Peet-a-wee, peet-a-wee, peet-a-wee
a cliff bird whines through the flying
earth-chilled fog. We are in a gully
surrounded by thicket pine that ply
their bark with white gum. Flat

spiles driven into tree gashes
drip with sap. My people, curled
in sleep, poke up like yellow
eggshells in grassy duckweed.
A mother sparrow fetches a cricket

treefrog while her young tittle in nightshade.
The snorting wingflaps of a sandhill
crane bark in awakening air. One
of my braves knaps a flint and sparks
flake off his hammerstone. Woodchips

flame their girdling as green logs
spit like hognose snakes. This
morning we cross the Great River for lands
to the west. The gored ground black
tips my ash splint. Opening a mocuck

sewed with stiff willow struts I see
we have only a few bullheads and creek
chubs for food. The spirits of squash rinds
and bean hulls and samp have long since
gone into flesh. A ringneck pheasant startles

his colors in goatmud at the riverbank.
The eye pools of the joining Bad Axe
peer at me like raccoons. The fog,
our fear, settles tightly down, unlifting.
We wait for our rising blood.

Finally women, children and men break
for the river, the wide, free water.
From a close distance white soldiers
sprint from trees and begin firing
on our people. Having only four canoes
for my tribe of one hundred sixty, many
turned at water's edge to fight,
some with only stones to hurl.
Squaws stripped treebark and in
the hollows placed their babies to
float them across. Being greatly
outnumbered some began swimming
to the west side. Six white men in a

longboat met them halfway and shot
the women, overturned the floating
children and clubbed all those they
could. A few of my people reached
the other shore, but Sioux warriors, our
tribal enemy, tomahawked them as
they crawled from the water like drowning
rats. The horrid sight of this massacre
wounded me deeply and with as many

of my people as could be gathered, I made
for the cover of woods. The dying
screams of my people split the darkening
fog in my heart. O father mercy.

In the future nights our dreams bring
to us, the breathing air will thicken
with blood and we breath it and drink it
and eat it. We cast our bodies on water

and from our height of poling flesh
our spears poise ready to leap
into the limitless dark dreams of water.
Sheaves of pain we will drag up

in handfuls. Standing, trolling from
the stiff white corpses our feet
become under water we search
for the first empty cry that breaks

the surface in ripples like flesh folds.
The fish of our hands spike their thorny
fins and the bobbing childflesh of
our children bloat like dead eyeballs.

Father, we weep, father, O sacred
spirit of life close the vision you
have opened to us. We snag our dead.
The casting hooks of our words

float into black day. Along dark shining
riverbottom stumps open their graves.
Our matted fur reddens. Our limbs
jump off in teethmarks. Silent water,

warm sway, the fluid stream of desires,
draws in, draws in, heavies our lungs,
our driftlog bodies turn free in water
and spinning, slowly turning in

their dark currents, bend and vanish.
Alone in the dark past, all light is red.
The blushing river climbs out its veins
and listening like a heart for a next

beat, I wait and wait and dream
I cannot die, but must take spears
and arrows into me like children I
will never give birth to, only swell

huge in disease with sharp life and wait
on riverbanks for floating forms we
do not recognize, then like a rat
hungry with rot, nibble, nibble, my flesh.

Dream of the Dead Warrior

The bronze moon notched
on night's wall, an old ivory tusk
is turning like an ear.
Underfoot, down where we put them

they move, shambling legbones
scraping bent nooks of arms and ribbed
fingers. In the buzzing
ground their nails rise like air bubbles.

Toadstones knock in arm sockets.
Their hollow eyes have seen us.
They are climbing up tree roots,
animal tunnels are stretching

to pass them. The shallow earth
rolls, they push through and flapping
like shadows they follow us.
We go deeper into the night

where our empty breaths
blinking like fireflies lead us.
Bushes snag our skin and we leave
ourselves slowly like red

flowers but do not stop.
Clacking in the wind
leaves hurl their flat hands at us.
Wind is lifting the ground and trees

have thickened into a wall.
We claw at low branches and rising
softly like rain
lift ourselves. We sink

into the wood. Other hands touch
our feet, wet tongues and eyeflesh
touch our legs. We climb higher into
the dark wind, squirrels

rattling spindly branches. The moon so close
is an open wound in our sides.
We reach the top tips and our arms
reach still for branches invisible

as veins against the sky blacker
than the dried blood of our bodies.
We cannot stop, only a pause
the pierce of recognition and we fall

rocking gently like a hammock
we fall toward the patient bronze smile
we fall into our open bones
waiting to receive us like lovers.

Song

This winter day
is alive in your eyes
and the brown pools
sluff with lazy snow.
Under our feet catfish

wibble in iced shadows.
Our tindered steps are slow
and my slack speech bares
swelled feelings. In my chest
you are swooping and I can only

stare, an awkward mute. There is so
much we see in others
but to ourselves is hidden.
We tumble down a tree
freckled hillside like skittled squirrels

and as our arched hips tangle
we lose our fear
of what the chilled ground
can do to unprotected bodies.
Below us a little way, the ground

is warm and where snow has not
yet sent its ashen fingers we curl together.
The mist of our mingled breath
is like the spray of waterfalls
and the day I first took you

to the cave behind the falling
river, my fingers flowed the channels
of your flesh and we tucked
safely into brown cleft banks.
How the fever enters us again,

I hunch on a cliff
and imagine us dying looped
around each other overturning
and when we reach that last instant
I do not know how we keep a sliver

of breath. We come back on crow
tracks unfamiliar to ourselves
afraid of what a simple madness
must seem. The tapping of a woodpecker
or forest animal brings us to the cold

naked glow of where we lie and so
I hitch your deerskin and we lumber off
in bearfur. The separate movement
of our feet and hands lopside our steps.
You are not my woman. I cannot

shake free of you or let you leave.
Drifts along the path hump up like graves.
In these we will hide our bodies
until seasons pass and our bones
melt in a new sun.

Losing a Son

Possessed of nakedness he has entered
a new nakedness and his bright
skin reaches to me like the hand

of a dead oak shaking the formless
night wind. Under the skin
of his skin pebbled for some

unknowing movement he watches
me watch him. I would share
in his ceremony, his vision

of pain, if only his
finger would rise up
like a striking snake and prick

my arm. Red slashes of a burning
plant cross his belly beltlike.
Hovering my spread fingers

over the heat, my hands curl
into my arms and the powers
inside my son fly flashing,

invisible to all except when the light
of fires splits the sky and storms
descend and find their way to form

smacking air against air to enter
the spaces between the space,
to enter the cool limbs of a child.

How helpless I stand in my shadow.
What a man will do for another
man who does not know the way of children

who cannot take up the soft flesh
and bear it on his backbone to the sacred
places deep inside and let the bite

of foxfire smoke pluck at his flat eyeball
or reach into the inner darkness
of a cave and find some damp thing growing.

Beyond the outward ticking rhythm
of life there is a solid winged
dream that flaps the breeze or

twirls the hard nippled hand of a man.
What open longing hung on my chest
like a wounded lung will fill with breath?

I will make a bier with the whitest
sweetbirch wood and place you, my son,
to my breast and with the blue sky

our awaiting friend, a larger fire than your
own will take us in her arms
and the singing leaves and sticks

will clap like hands and we will burn
in the flames of our sorrow.

At the River

Through the trees
past plums wagging in the wind
and patches of blood juleps
scattered in small villages

around a narrow plank of water
to the brown shallow river
I come. Over the frost
spume of the river, far

past the other bank and into the blending
forest that touches the sky's
edge toward the home
lands of our people I send

my eyes. From the first dawn
of the first moon the wise
light has given life, the food
of fields and the friendly rain.

Now, we have left our homes
like the butterfly bringing
nothing, not touching
the ground, blown in the direction

of the wind. Our enemy
is ourselves. The crops
we have grown are fear
and hate. The night loon

is our brother calling
to his brother. Crows have spread
their wings and they become
our arms. Our campfires grow

to ashes. Our bodies become clay.
The salt of my tongue turns red
with the blood of all my lost people.
My feet sink

prickled into the dead
mud of the riverbank.
Flat footprints of the sky
float stationary like fluid

driftwood ruffled by the gentle
swash of water. A carp
flaps the surface. Cross
hatching a coiled eddy

an otter blinks then sails
into a cave. The song
of the river is like a heart
that no one can stop.

It follows its path
unopposed to a still
larger river past the home
of the Winnebago and then

to the Fox. It is the father
of our children and their children,
and it sends to us children
of its own. It lays its head

on the flow of seasons, grows
and sheds new skin as the snake,
it gives fish to its friends,
no tribe claims it, no man can.

We have left the bones
of our fathers, we have lost
their spirits. In the morning
we wake to the same sun.

This day our eyes will fall
like trees into memory
and this river will carry
me to my home.

Song of Return

The way this roselily wind
spars my upbound breath
and sun dash of smokeless flame

around my rock-straddling legs,
while trees shake free
of their colored cloaks

my head bursts like a pouting
weasel bud. A man alone in age
untames the forest wilds of marrow,

dense in the overhanging, tucked-in
body flesh. I have come home
to die, to take the dew sprinkles

my uncut days stretch out
and wrap under their final
blanket. My sorrows sink shaped

like unturned riverstones. Under
the blue glaze of sky, foam skim
pops its old pains. My children

have split their eggshells and old
flights have died in their legs.
I know what I have always

known. The seeds of blood lost
in battle were always lost, only
the wind's sun-browned finger

tips move sure. My grasp,
my blind touch. Bee honey sticks
its shivery tongues to my hand,

the sweetness, the sweetness.
Balanced on my legs I have no
more people. My freedom lifts

its spidery thighs and the bone rattle
of stars behind the bright fleshy
day dance my death rhythm. A fire

somewhere lit in escaping passion
wails its light. Father, your
coming arms are warm. Sun flecks

pile their banks. Cold tinkering
bones kindle their haunches.
O father, your warm arms

send new heat. Dull breezes grind
their teeth and dry streams flow into
sandstone. All my tribes pass war whelps

into whimpering trees. At the honed edge
of this clearing the dead file of tree
shadows has begun. Processions of

mushrooms bow flatheads and I lift green
spears of grass from burning sheaths.
Come soon, come soon a spiny flycatcher

warbles. I watch my steps
lead me to the bluffs overlooking
the Great River. At this distance

the brown water is unmoving. Its
sleeping depths do not stretch their hands
to me. My height, my beckoning

bones, above the silent singing river
waver like the flame of butterfly wings
on this mountain, blink and blink, unnoticed.

The Passing of Ke-o-kuck

A chiseled awareness caught in blood
of fiery wings and when a man
rises from his grave of days and wind
speaks through his bones, nightskin
tears the growing light,

numb eyes shut on the land,
treading shadows pulse the buried dead.
Beyond solid cold the sun
casts up veins of dragging grief
and strikes the air like clouds of stone.

Prayers bobbed on the sour mouth
of night hang like wretched winter birds.
The solitary flame wraps its eye on barbs
and roots curl in their trees.
Bristles of fibers withdraw

the light of shade and more alive
than ever, driven by eyes, the center
of eyes, whirling toward the long night
of descent, toward the ceiling of sky
in flow of terror that cannot pass but remains,

remains to foul and rend
the eyes of land and blood
in the wings of the one wind.
Speak through my bones.

The morning lies down like a shroud.
The moon has turned a black cheek.
It is the climbing fall.
My men rise from out my breath.

Unto His Fathers

And my people brought Pyesa
to a sheltered burialground
in a forest grove and as we
gave my father back to the earth
I spoke the words of Na-na-ma-kee

be as the birds of the air and trust how far
your wings will carry you

raise up children on the seeds of the wind
and bend with the breath of seasons

carry the heart of others in your arms and know
the weight of trust

plant firm feet in sun and shade, accept the touch
of nature's reason

follow the road to the mountains, many paths lead
to the top

tread lightly the fields of others, their crops
must also grow and reach for light

draw power from storms and natural violence,
you are the energy in the veins of earth

all living things touch the air and waters for life,
the family of man is a brother to every creature

nurture the seedling and the dying oak, the smallest
streams hold the magic of stars

we are a small tribe in the heavens, all children
are the moons of time and the suns of eternity

then I went off
into the woods
and cleared my vision
with weeping.

The Speech of Trees

In sandscrabble night
watch of trees my breath
clucks like a knotholed wind.
I sniff the air of wood, the vision,
and open trees to my body.

In my hole of night I see
the forest move, the voices
of its rhythmic pitter. Bulrush
and sedge cling to me. Wattle
stitches its twigs to my twigs

and bluebell, mayflower,
hackberry and shooting star tremble
in their child march. Stars wink
and sprinkle deer tails that vanish
in a vast forest of sky.

My ground hackles scrape their wooden
knuckles while down where things
are lost to light, I feel the secret
shifting of soil. Withering roots
comb the earth for family bones,

the charred, scorched rib sickles
of ancestors. Unseen ways slow
babbling language. The thousand tongues
of my leaves relax and pause.
Tasting in my bark the weariness

of seasons, I repeat my scars, unable
to clear these black lightning branches.
In the boughs of day we cannot
stop the winters turning on us,
the image we call our own. Blooms

of my sons cannot remake
themselves. Coming through the night
air, riding their days like ancient ponies,
my people pass. In the cage of my trunk,
no one calls out. The last spatters

of youth blood bury their heads.
I am alone with the speech of trees.
Phrases grow and die in my hand,
in the still palm of life,
that takes up the shape no mother

could fashion. Seeking the wall
black as death, not to enter but to approach,
for the knowledge of position, of boundary,
of where it stands my root ends back
toward the light that does not reach,

I clamber, expand, like the dreams of stone.
I leave my tunnels in shadow,
the empty smell of root sprouts and humus
and earth loam. My flowering hands
are dragging out their green. Cordworms

ripen like berries and locusts cackle
and sputter their messages. I bark
my new speech, the words unpegging
meaning in natural, unfamiliar fall.
The groggy tongues stumble, then leap

from mouth to mouth. My rampant colors
splay and peal. Fuming in my splendor
I do not feel the gentle fibers tug
for life or choke the thickening roots
in the moist poison of their soil, and die.

Dream of Eagles

In the mild sky eagles
stir the blue like clouds.
They are eagles.

Grey lights behind their eyes
return the pale suns of my skin.
Head feathers, eagle plumes flower

my back in their neat rows,
two abreast, aloft in white, perfect
flight. Our brotherhood is not complete,

but it is a brotherhood. In the cloth
of feather color is purpose. The sag
of my arms attach the brown, the white.

The thought of movement, of flight
passes their eyes. The long, slow
dance of their swoops make them

look caught on spider strands or
the hidden hands of wind, effortless.
The eagles are closer now, I can see

wing cords pull and release,
pull and release, the motion of rivers
against the shorebank. Against the light

they are hands, unattached, fluid,
gentle in descent. The gliding breeze
is a spring breeze, full of planting

and wild mint and lilac blooms.
On my stone tower of mountain above
the Great River I am close to eagles,

and their dance around the fire blaze
of sun is the eagle dance, the joining
dance, and on the wingtips are prayers

my people offer to heavens, to spirits.
More graceful than the fall of snow,
I think eagles must live in sky,

braid their nests in clouds and never
touch the weight of earth. Finally,
my feathers rustle in the windless air

above the sorrow, the grief of trees
and grass and all that move in earth.
Like a breath, my wings stretch clear

lungs, again, again, and drawing
in, pressing out, lift this sack
of flesh, the bone frame,

the dream. In the beak and eyes
of each eagle, my braves, my tribe,
accepting their chief whose blood was red,

whose skin was red, now white, but
of the eagle, not the false white of men.
My useless legs drop off like tombs.

Rising, our flight becomes smoke
and our white is turning to blue,
the blue of our fathers. The sound

of past days leaves me and streaking
into the pure blue, quiet final womb,
first womb, someone is weeping,
weeping, for my people, my people.